BIRCH
BOOKS

First published by Birch Books 2020

ISBN (978-81-949495-1-0)

Email : books.birch@gmail.com

THE MOUSETRAP

RUCHIRA DARDA

For my sons Aryaveer and Adhiraj, whose demands for stories made me spin tales every night and whose giggles and chuckles have made bedtime special forever.

For my mum, who chiseled the best out of me.

Em, the farm mouse's favourite hour of the day is when the sun rises to kiss the sky. He puts on his purple waistcoat and feels absolutely royal. In the same spirit, he leaves his mouse hole every morning to go to the farmer's kitchen.

At 10:00 am each day, the farmer's wife would begin preparing for lunch and would spill some scrumptious pieces of fresh cheese and vegetables on the kitchen floor. Em would only need to pick up a slice of warm bread off the rack and he would be good to go. Unfortunately, this morning was more of a nightmare.

As usual, Em had gotten ready to leave his cozy mouse hole and had gotten himself **STUCK.**

He wondered how this could have happened. He only had a small piece of lasagna, some cake and a whole croissant for dinner last night.

He tried mighty hard to push himself out of that hole, but in vain.

One last attempt and then Em, half way through the door of his royal mouse hole, decided to give up.

"In a few hours, I will have skipped breakfast and lunch and I will surely slip right through" he thought.

He suddenly remembered that the farmer's wife was going to bake a cake for the farmer's birthday along with roast turkey and a side of mashed potatoes. While his face lit up temporarily, he soon realized it will be a while before he would be able to taste turkey again.

Em spotted Gloria the goat in the distance. He called out to her for help. Gloria snickered at Em's story at first and then looked around for a way to help. She saw the farmer's rope, which he used to tie hay together, kept on the floor. “Hold on to it and I will pull you out”, exclaimed Gloria. “1, 2, 3, here we go.”

The rope gave way,
Gloria went crashing into the haystack at the back and Em stayed exactly where he was. **STUCK.**

"Don't worry, Em. I will go and get some help", claimed a disappointed Gloria. In a few minutes, Gloria returned with Ram, the dashing ram of the farm. Ram lowered his large horns for Em to hold on to but it was pointless. His horns were beyond a mouse's grip. His tiny paws couldn't possibly hold on to them.

Gloria then approached the extremely sharp Harsh, the horse for help.

Harsh and Gloria seemed to be discussing the farm mouse's situation for a while and then walked away.

"Hey, hey fellas, where are you going? Don't leave me like this...please come back!" cried a desperate Em.

In that moment of silence,
a shiver ran down Em's spine.

“Is that Billa I hear?” In the distance you could hear the soft purr of a cat that was approaching its prey with caution.

"This is the silliest way to die, you can't make it that easy for him god. Get me out of here!"

Before he could even fathom the possibility of an escape, Em was out of that hole in one strong push full of determination; like a slab of butter would glide over warm toast.

"AHA! Now where is that Billa?", he boldly challenged.

"Hahahaha!!!",
guffawed Gloria and Harsh. "A small prank to help a friend, hope you didn't mind?",
Gloria asked politely.

“Uh hmm, not at all, but don't do that again, okay!”, said an embarrassed Em. “Now, if you'll excuse me, I have to make it to the farmer's kitchen before lunch is served.”

Off went the farm mouse to relish
a much deserved afternoon feast.

ABOUT THE AUTHOR

Ruchira Darda is a parent to two inspiring young children. They spend time together weaving stories and exploring the world through them.

Ruchira has a decade of experience working with children via her children's enrichment centre - The Yellow Door. Her pursuit of spirituality is the purpose behind her storytelling. She is an expert on personalities and is a sought after Relationship and Parenting Coach. Her quest for spirituality coupled with her experience with women and children has led her to simplfying her learnings for children.

While she believes spiritual learning should come to children from a young age she also believes that everything we say to our children doesn't need to be so structured. That's why her storytelling is a blend of spurts of laughter, tamed with a dose of goodness.